Cotswolds & Forest of Dean Travel Guide

Attractions, Eating, Drinking, Shopping & Places To Stay

Christopher Reed

Copyright © 2014, Astute Press
All Rights Reserved.

No part of this publication may be reproduced, stored in a retrieval system, or transmitted, in any form or by any means without the prior written permission of the publisher, nor be otherwise circulated in any form of binding or cover other than that in which it is published and without similar condition being imposed on the subsequent purchaser.

If there are any errors or omissions in copyright acknowledgements the publisher will be pleased to insert the appropriate acknowledgement in any subsequent printing of this publication.

Although we have taken all reasonable care in researching this book we make no warranty about the accuracy or completeness of its content and disclaim all liability arising from its use

Table of Contents

Cotswolds 7
   Culture 10
   Location & Orientation 11
   Climate & When to Visit 13

Sightseeing Highlights 14
   Broadway Tower 14
   St. Mary's Church 16
   Corinium Museum 18
   Cotswold Water Park 19
   Cotswold Motoring Museum & Toy Collection 20
   Cotswold Falconry Centre 22
   Blenheim Palace 24
   Gloucester Cathedral 25
   Cheltenham Spa Town 26
   Chipping Campden 29
   Nature & Gardens 31
      Batsford Aboretum & Wild Garden 31
      Birdland – Park & Gardens 31
      Clearwell Caves 31
      Cotswold Way National Trail 31
      Westonbirt – The National Arboretum 32
      Thermal Bath Spa 32
      Stratford Butterfly Farm 32
      Kenilworth Castle & Elizabethan Garden 32
   Historical Cathedrals & Castles 33
      Berkeley Castle 33
      Roman Baths 33
      Snowshill Manor & Garden 33
      Sudeley Castle 33
      Tewkesbury Abbey 34
   Museums & Others 34
      Out of the Hat 34
      Nature in Art 34
      Keith Harding's World of Mechanical Music 35

Recommendations for the Budget Traveller 37

- **Places to Stay** 37
  - Days Inn Michaelwood 37
  - The Old Stocks Hotel, Restaurant & Bar 38
  - Byfield House 39
  - The Battledown 40
  - The Ivy House 40
- **Places to Eat** 41
  - Piazza Fontana 41
  - Cutlers Restaurant 41
  - Lumiere Restaurant 42
  - Café Mosaic 42
  - Prithvi Restaurant 43
- **Places to Shop** 44
  - Highgrove Gardens 44
  - Bath Markets 44
  - Tewkesbury Markets 45
  - Stroud Markets 46
  - Cheltenham Markets 46

Forest of Dean & the Wye Valley 47
- Location & Orientation 49
- Climate & When to Visit 50

Sightseeing Highlights 51
- Forest of Dean 51
- Chepstow (Welsh: Cas-Gwent) 53
- Caerleon (Welsh: Caerllion) 54
- Tintern (Welsh: Tyndyrn) 55
- Abergavenny (Welsh: Y Fenni) 57
- Hereford 58
- Monmouth (Welsh: Trefynwy) 59
- Ross-on-Wye 61
- Usk (Welsh: Brynbuga) 63
- Gloucester 64

Recommendations for the Budget Traveller 67
- **Places to Stay** 67
  - Hotel Ibis Gloucester 67
  - Castle View Hotel 68
  - Riverside Hotel 68
  - Munstone House 69
  - Premier Inn 70
- **Places to Eat** 70

Warwick's Country Pub & Eatery 70
The Three Salmons..71
Na Lampang...72
N68 Bistro 72
Shangri-La 73
Places to Shop...73
Eastgate Shopping Centre 73
Stella Books 74
Labels Outlet Shopping...75
Ross Garden Store...75
Gloucestershire Arts & Crafts Centre 76

Cotswolds

The 'quintessentially English' Cotswolds is a gentle hilly countryside region of southcentral England. This popular tourist destination is spread over 790 square miles and is close to the cities of Gloucester, Bath, Oxford, and Stratford-upon-Avon. The Cotswolds has been designated an English 'Area of Outstanding Natural Beauty' (AONB) since 1966 and stretches across six counties (Gloucestershire, Oxfordshire, Warwickshire, Wiltshire, Somerset, and Worcestershire).

The Cotswolds is the largest of the forty AONBs in England and Wales and is the second largest protected landscape in England (after the Lake District National Park).

The Cotswolds region, famous for its honey-coloured limestone villages, medieval market places, numerous parks and wild gardens, and the beautiful rolling hills in the countryside, has become one of the major tourist attractions in the UK bringing in £1 billion to the local economy. In fact, tourism is the primary source of employment with over 20,000 jobs.

The Cotswolds draws tourists who are looking for a quiet getaway from the hustle and din of city life. The region has numerous walk and cycle trails including National and Regional Walking Routes like the 103-mile Cotswolds Way Trail, and the 146-mile Shakespeare's Way. The hills have numerous vantage points having magnificent views of the countryside. Two very popular points are the Broadway Tower and the Cleeve Hill – the highest point of the Cotswolds at 1083 ft (330m) above sea level.

There is no historic official record of the name Cotswolds, but it is generally believed that it got its name from the 12th century Anglo-Saxon chieftain named Cod who owned the highland or 'wold'. Codswolds over the years became Cotswolds. The region earned its wealth in the medieval ages from wool trade. In fact, so popular was the wool of Cotswolds that there was a 12th century saying - 'In Europe the best wool is English and in England the best wool is Cotswold'.

Monasteries and Abbeys used to raise sheep – known as the Cotswolds Lions for their big build and golden fleeces – in the hills. The money they earned was often used to build churches which popularly came to be known as 'wool churches'. In fact, so high was the production of wool, that the monarchy passed Acts to push the use of wool beyond cloth-making and to make sure that the importance of wool remained intact. The Acts, called the Buried in Wool Acts 1667 & 1668 required all bodies to be buried in wool (or woolen products) only, unless the person died of a natural disease, like plague. The Acts were repealed in 1814. The Cotswolds region is also believed to have been a major Salt Route. Salt was used for dyes as well as medicines, making it an important commodity of trade. Winchcombe was at a crossroads for the salt trade routes that allowed the aristocracy to earn huge sums from the taxes levied. 2 other industries were established in the Cotswolds region but never took off as expected – silk production and tobacco. Silk Lane and Tobacco Close (street) in Winchcombe can still be seen as stark reminders of these failed industries.

Today tourism in Cotswolds has a lot to offer beyond just the magnificent views of its countryside. In fact, tourism is promoted in Cotswolds with the catchphrase – 'The Cotswolds More Than Just A View'. There are a number of popular destinations in the Cotswolds region that include Cheltenham, Cirencester, Stroud, Winchcombe, Tetbury, and Stow-on-the-Wold. Spread across the different regions are numerous villages dating back to the 15th and 16th centuries that have remained almost unchanged over the centuries.

Many of the buildings in this region are built with Oolitic Limestone, a natural building material that was found in abundance. The buildings are now 'grade listed' by the UK government, so no structural changes are allowed, thus retaining their original form. There are also many castles, museums, sporting events, festivals, and leisure activities in Cotswolds. The numerous family attractions and low cost options have made Cotswolds an irresistible tourist attraction in the UK.

Culture

Whether it's summer or winter, there is always a festival or two listed in the Cotswolds calendar. From comedy to crafts, and from baking to battles, there is a wide variety of festivals and fairs in the different regions of Cotswolds.

Theatre lovers can book a show at the Everyman Theatre or Playhouse Theatre, or attend the Open Air Theatre Festival in July at Cheltenham. For the lovers of poetry and literature, there are the Camden Literature Festival and the Cheltenham Poetry Festival during early summer. Music lovers are spoilt for choice, and, quite rightly so. The hills have inspired many British composers and their compositions – Herbert Howells' Piano Quartet in A Minor and Gustav Holst's The Cotswolds, to name a couple. The Cheltenham Folk Festival, Lechlade Music Festival, Winchcombe Festival of Music and Arts, Rhythm and Blues Festival (Gloucester), and Tetbury Music Festival are just a few of the festivals that keep music lovers engaged and enthralled all the year round.

Events like the Olimpick Games at Chipping Campden, the Cheese Rolling at Coopers Hill, the Cliffords Circus, and Football on the River at Bourton-on-the-Water are family attractions for the adults and kids alike. Christmas Markets are the toast-of-the-town in a number of Cotswolds towns in December.

Festivals and fairs are not limited to arts and sports in Cotswolds. The Food and Drink Festivals in Cheltenham and Lechlade, the Garden Party at Gloucester Quays, the Lavender Flower Season, the Hat Festival at Gloucester, or the Cotswold Festival Battle Re-enactment at Stow-on-the-Wold provide the visitors and locals with a wide variety of festivals to choose from.

Location & Orientation

The Cotswolds region is barely 100 miles from London, and less than 50miles from Birmingham and Leeds. Although London is the closest major city with multiple airports (Heathrow – IATA: LHR; Gatwick – IATA: LGW; London City – IATA: LCY; Luton – IATA: LTN; Stansted – IATA: STN), visitors can also choose to fly into the Birmingham Airport (IATA:BHX) or Bristol Airport (IATA:BRS). The London Heathrow Airport is directly connected to the Cotswolds region through coach service run by National Express. Those opting for the train can take a direct connection too; the train goes via London Paddington Station in central London.

Train connections for the 90 minute journey to the Cotswolds region are available from London Paddington Station daily every hour. Ticket costs about £20 if bought a week in advance. Train connections are not available to all the towns in the Cotswolds region; connecting stations are at Oxford, Hanborough, Kingham, Moreton-in-Marsh, Stratford-upon-Avon, Cheltenham, Gloucester, Stroud, Kemble, Chippenham, and Bath. Details of train schedules and fares are available at: http://www.thetrainline.com/ & http://www.nationalrail.co.uk/.

The Cotswolds is connected by road through a coach (bus) service run by the National Express - http://www.nationalexpress.com/home.aspx. The coaches start from Victoria Coach Station in London and takes about 3.5 hours to reach the Cotswolds. The coaches stop at many major points including Oxford, Bourton-on-the-Water, Cheltenham, Northleach, Chippenham, Bath, Gloucester, Moreton-in-Marsh, Stow-on-the-Wold, Stratford-upon-Avon, and Stroud. A typical journey booked about a week in advance would cost £17.

For those arriving at the train station or airport, taxi service would be needed to get from the terminal to the hotel as the bus service in the Cotswolds region is very infrequent. There are very few connections and buses often ply once in an hour. Taxi service in the various towns of Cotswolds can be found at: http://www.cotswold.gov.uk/nqcontent.cfm?a_id=1041&tt=cotswold.

Once in the Cotswolds region, the best way to move around town is walking. There are a number of walk trails in the hills that provide magnificent views. The region also has a number of cycle paths - http://www.cotswold.gov.uk/nqcontent.cfm?a_id=2626&tt=cotswold. As stated earlier, bus service is infrequent so if one is planning to move from one town to another, it is best to pre-book a taxi or drive. Car hire is available at Bath, Cheltenham, and Oxford costing about £60 per day. (Note: One can even take the 2-hr drive from London taking the M4 or M40 motorway) Although the regular car rentals are available (Avis & Hertz), one can also hire a classic Jaguar for the trip at http://www.classicmotoring.co.uk/. Couples on a romantic getaway can also try driving the famous Romantic Road route - http://www.the-cotswolds.org/top/english/seeanddo/romanticroad/index.php.

Climate & When to Visit

Not only are the hills of Cotswolds very English, so is the weather. A mild climate with occasional rainfall is predominant the whole year. Temperatures touch the high 20s (in Celsius) in the summer with the lows in the low teens. Winters are cooler with the temperature in single digits. Months of lowest rainfall are between April and July. This mild temperate climate attracts tourists all the year round especially during Autumn and Spring.

Sightseeing Highlights

Broadway Tower

Broadway Village (Near A44 motorway)
Worcestershire
Tel: 01386 852 390
http://www.broadwaytower.co.uk/

Standing 17m high on the Broadway Hill near the village of Broadway in Worcestershire, the Broadway Tower is a folly at 213m above sea level making it the 2nd highest point in the Cotswolds ridge, 2nd only to Cleeve Hill (330m above sea level).

The 'Saxon' Tower is on the 'Cotswolds Way Walk' and provides a spectacular view of the rolling hills of the region. On a clear day, one can see an expanse of 62 miles radius covering 16 counties! The view includes Vales of Evesham and Gloucester, and across the Severn valley up to the Welsh Mountains.

The Broadway Tower, constructed in 1799, is a Gothic folly designed by James Wyatt resembling a mock castle. The building of the Tower was commissioned and sponsored by George William, the 6th Earl of Coventry. It was his wife's – Lady Coventry's – curiosity that led to the building of the tower as she wondered if a beacon on a tower could be seen from her home – the Croome Court – 12 miles away from the Broadway Hill. The beacon could be seen clearly. The Tower, in the later years housed the printing press of Sir Thomas Phillipps, 1st Baronet and a renowned antiquary and book collector. It was also a summer retreat of pre-Raphaelite artist William Morris.

The Tower, which has featured in many TV series and films, including Sherlock Holmes and The Gemini Factor, can be reached through the Cotswolds Way at Fish Hill. One can also go for the steeper climb through the Broadway Village. The Morris Hall in the Tower has exhibitions highlighting the history of the Tower and its surrounding landscape.

Tickets to the Tower costs: Adult – £4.80; Child (10 – 14yrs) – £3; Family Ticket (with a maximum of 2 adults) – £13.

The Tower is open daily from 10:00 am – 5:00 pm.

St. Mary's Church

The Lychgate, Stroud Road
Painswick, Gloucestershire
Tel: 01452 814 795
http://stmaryspainswick.org.uk

Painswick, located in Gloucestershire, is a village and a civil parish (the lowest tier in the government) best known for the Late Baroque (Rococo) gardens and the parish churches. The village with about 8000 inhabitants is often referred to as the Queen of the Cotswolds for its natural beauty. Dominating the skyline of the Painswick village is the St Mary's Painswick, part of the Beacon Benefice in the Church of England. The Church is a Grade I listed building and is believed to have been built in the early 11th century by Ernesi, a rich Anglo-Saxon nobleman.

Over the next few centuries, the Church changed hands from one family to another. Damaged by lightning, fire, and bullet and cannon-shots, it went through many restorations over the centuries. The nave and the pointed perpendicular tower were built in the 15th century. The 17th and 18th centuries saw the addition of a number of galleries in the north and south aisles. Bells were added to the Tower in the 16th century but were replaced in 1731. Today there are 14 bells, most of those from the 18th century that have never been tuned since their installation reflecting the quality of craftsmanship.

The highlights of the church are the yew trees and the tombs in its courtyard. By tradition, the Church is said to have exactly 99 yew trees as it is believed that the 100th tree would be uprooted by the devil. (However, interestingly there are 103 yew trees in the courtyard today, and there are 100 yew trees in the plan of the Church leaflet itself.) The 33 tombs of varying shapes and sizes spread across the courtyard, and seem to be guarded by the yew trees. All the tombs are of the wealthy merchants and businessmen of that region except one, tomb number 32, which is of John Bryan, the creator of many of the tombs and altarpieces of the Church.

Tours are available to the top of the Tower. Dress codes are enforced and one has to be reasonably fit to climb the 90 steps and walk round the parapet. Children below 8 and individual tours are not allowed; there has to be a group of 5 – 6 people. (Individuals can wait to join another group) There is no entry fee but a donation of £20 for 6 people is taken.

Tours are on Fridays and Saturdays every half hour from 11:30 am – 4:30 pm (and till 1:30 pm on Saturday)

Also See in Painswick: The early 18th century Rococo Gardens

Corinium Museum

Park Street,
Cirencester
Tel: 01285 655 611
http://coriniummuseum.org/

Established in 1938, this multi award-winning museum is famous for its Roman collections dating back to the 2nd century. The Museum got its name from the town it is located in – Cirencester – which was Corinium to the Romans. The Museum has a wide collection of Roman artifacts relating to their society and everyday life. There are a few interactive sections including one where a visitor can dress up as a Roman warrior or meet an Anglo-Saxon Princess. 2 of the most important collections of the Museum are the Four Seasons and Hunting Dogs mosaics that were excavated in the mid 19th century. The excavations also triggered an interest in archeological findings in Cirencester that included the basilica excavations in 1897 and the Union Workhouse excavations in 1922. Most of the Roman objects were excavated from the Roman town of Corinium Dobunnorum.

The Museum has over 1 million objects and is in a process of listing those online. The collections date from the 2nd century up to the Victorian period in the 19th century. Presently, 60000 objects from the collection can be searched and viewed online. The Museum hosts a variety of exhibitions ranging from handicrafts to paintings and drawings. It also hosts workshops like 'Making a Mask' and 'Roman Saddles'. Evenings are often reserved for film shows (ticket prices separate).

Ticket prices for Museum entry costs: Adult – £5; Child – £2.50

The Corinium Museum is open 10:00 am – 5:00 pm from Mon – Sat, and 2:00 pm – 5:00 pm on Sundays.

Cotswold Water Park

Gloucestershire/Wiltshire
Tel: 01793 752 413 (Cotswold Water Park Trust)
http://www.waterpark.org/
http://www.cotswoldcountrypark.co.uk/

Spread across 40 sq miles in the counties of Wiltshire, Gloucestershire, and West Oxfordshire, the Cotswold Water Park with 150 lakes is the UK's largest marl (calcium carbonate mixed with various amounts of clay and silt) lake system. It has 74 fishing lakes and over 93 miles of walkways and cycling paths. The Park has 6000 years of habitation and is a favourite with bird watchers and nature lovers. So popular are the sightings that one can go to the blogging website - http://cotswoldwaterpark.wordpress.com/ - and list the sighting along with the date. The Park was created with 60 years of gravel extraction that were later filled naturally. The Park area encompasses 14 villages with 20000 residents who live and work there.

With numerous water activities like fishing, boating, skiing, swimming, and kayaking, the Park has become a top tourist attraction with half a million visitors every year. One can also try camping, paintballing, shooting, horse riding, rally driving, golf, or cycling in one of its trails. There is also a popular beach that is open Feb – Dec and is the largest inland beach in the UK. Enquiry about the beach can be made at Cotswold Country Park and Beach – Tel: 01285 868 096.

The Water Park is owned by a number of businesses (and individuals) and is managed by the Cotswold Water Park Trust. The Trust was set up in 1996 and aims to deliver on 4 parameters – Access, Conservation, Leisure, and Education. The Trust can be contacted directly for specific queries on the Park at: Cotswold House, Manor Farm, Cirencester GL7 5QF (Email – info@waterpark.org).

The park is open all the year round. There is a £5 entry charge for adults; children enter for free. Activities and food in the Park are managed by different businesses and each has separate individual charges.

Cotswold Motoring Museum & Toy Collection

The Old Mill, Bourton-on-the-Water, Gloucestershire
Tel: 01451 821 255
http://www.cotswoldmotoringmuseum.co.uk/

Founded in 1978 by car enthusiast Mike Cavanagh.

The Cotswold Motoring Museum & Toy Collection is a must for car lovers for its exciting collection of automobiles of the 20th century. In 1999, the Museum was taken over by the non-profit organization – Civil Service Motoring Association (CMSA). Housed in a Grade II listed refurbished 18th century watermill by the River Windrush, this 7500 sq ft Museum has 7 showrooms displaying dozens of cars and motorbikes, and a unique toy collection all the year round. The Museum has won a number of awards, notably, 'Museum of the Year 2011' by Classic Car Weekly, Visitor Attraction of the Year 2003 by Heart of England Tourist Board, and the Museums and Heritage Award 2004 for their interpretation project "Big Ideas for Small Children".

The collection in the Museum ranges from cars and motorbikes, to caravans and motoring memorabilia. Amongst the notable vintage car collections are the Austin Swallow (1930) and the Morris Minor (1935). The latest car in the Museum is the 1972 Mini Clubman. The motorcycle collection includes a 1920 Indian V Twin, a 1934 Levis, and a 1919 ABC Motorized Scooter. The collection also includes a 1936 Brough Superior – also known as the 'widow maker' for the number of fatalities due to its high speed; the most notable being Laurence of Arabia. The collection also includes children's favourite Brum, television's supercar hero.

The unique motor Toy Collection can transport the elderly to their childhood days with its wide variety of pedal cars and toys. The Austin pedal car or the rocking horse is sure to bring back nostalgia to many. There are also toy boats, model aeroplanes, and bicycles. The Collection not only includes one-off models made by manufacturers but also homemade toys and models.

The Memorabilia Collection includes practical items like brake fluid tins and spark plugs. The Vintage Collection has an interesting mix of exhibits that include vintage clothing, hand-operated pumps, and a set of 1920s art deco racing car teapots.

Entry charges to the Museum are: Adult – £4.75; Child (4 – 16 years) £3.40; Family of maximum 2 adults – £14.95

The Museum is open daily from Feb – Nov between 10:00 am & 6:00 pm. Opening and closing dates of the season are posted on the website.

Cotswold Falconry Centre

Batsford Park, Moreton-in-Marsh
Gloucestershire
Tel: 01386 701 043
http://www.cotswold-falconry.co.uk/

The Cotswold Falconry Centre with its wide variety of birds of prey has become a top tourist attraction of the Cotswolds region attracting over 20000 visitors every year. It was started in 1988 with 150 birds of prey and over the years, about 30 separate new species have been bred in the falconry. Free flight demonstrations are given of some of these birds of prey, and there are a number of tours specific to some of the birds.

The falconry is also a breeding ground for many birds. One can walk in the Owl Woods trail where a natural habitat has been created to make the birds of prey feel as if they are in their natural environment. For the visitors, it is a rare opportunity to watch the natural breeding behaviour of these birds at close proximity.

Displays are held in the summer time at 11:30, 1:30, 3:00, and 4:00pm where the free flying vultures, owls, falcons, caracaras, and eagles soar into the clouds in their own typical style. The Flying Start Tour is a 60 minute guided tour where visitors are given the opportunity to handle different birds of prey. One can also fly a hawk as a part of the tour. Weekday tours are scheduled at 10:30am, 12:30pm, 2:00pm, and 3:30pm. Special Weekend Tour details are posted on the website. The Tour is priced at £40 for 1 person and £60 for 2. The Owl Evening Tour starts at 6:30 in the evening. Visitors get a chance to not only get acquainted with the different kinds of owls in the Centre; they also have the opportunity to handle some of the owls. The Tour costs £45 person and includes hot drinks. The most thrilling and day long tour at the Centre is the Eagle Day Tour. Visitors get to handle a majestic Golden Eagle and then enjoy the thrill of flying an eagle too. The 6.5 hr Tour starts at 10:00am and includes lunch for 2 people. The Tour is priced at £250 for 2 people.

The Falconry Centre is open from Feb – Nov. (Dates for the season are posted on the website) Ticket prices for entry to the Centre are: Adult – £8, Child – £4, Family with maximum 2 adults – £20.

Blenheim Palace

Woodstock, Oxfordshire
Tel: 01993 815 600
http://www.blenheimpalace.com/

The Blenheim Palace is the only building in England with the title of palace that did not belong to the Royal family or did not have an Episcopal (pertaining to a Bishop) authority.

The grand country house built in the first quarter of the 18th century was the residence of the dukes of Marlborough. The English Baroque styled building, one of the largest houses in England, has been a World Heritage Site since 1987. It has another claim to fame – it is the birthplace and ancestral home of Sir Winston Churchill and has been home to the Churchill family for 300 years. It is located in Woodstock which is about 8 miles from Oxford.

The palace was a gift from Queen Anne to the 1st Duke of Marlborough – John Churchill – for winning the battle of Blenheim in 1704 against the French and the Bavarians. The Palace, built in the English Baroque style, has grand state rooms with stunning craftsmanship. The Palace is surrounded by a 2100-acre parkland and the beautifully maintained Pleasure Gardens and Formal Gardens. There is also beautiful lake in the property. The Estate supports a number of businesses, most notably the Blenheim Palace Natural Mineral Water. There are also a number of leisure and family activities in the Palace grounds including a maze, adventure playground, mini train, and butterfly house.

Combo ticket prices for the Palace, Park & Gardens are: Adult – £22, Child – £12. Ticket prices for only the Park & Gardens are: Adult – £13, Child – £6.50. Concession and Family Tickets are also available. Note: There is no refund for tickets bought online.

Gloucester Cathedral

12 College Green, Gloucester
Gloucestershire
Tel: 01452 528 095
http://www.gloucestercathedral.org.uk/

Cathedral Church of St Peter and the Holy and Indivisible Trinity, popularly known as the Gloucester Cathedral was constructed in the last quarter of the 11th century in the northern part of the city of Gloucester. Regarded as one of the most beautiful buildings in Northern Europe, it is a mix of Romanesque, Gothic, and Norman architecture. Located at the heart of the city, the Cathedral is the only location outside London where a monarch was coroneted – Henry III in 1216. The cathedral has stained glass windows with 14th century etchings of golf and (presumed) football – some of the earliest records of these games in the world! Harry Potter fans have seen the insides of the Cathedral a number of times as it was the film location of the Hogwarts School!

The foundation of the Church was laid in 1089 by Abbot Serlo. Over the next 400 years numerous extensions and restorations were done to the Cathedral. Due to the changing architectural style in England during these centuries, the cathedral carries a unique mix of the different styles – the columns are Romanesque, the nave is Norman, and the south porch is Gothic. The Cathedral is 130m long with a Tower rising to 68.6m.

Notable attractions in the Gloucester Cathedral include 46 14th-century misericords, canopied shrine of King Edward II of England, and the fan vault cloisters – the oldest in the UK.

Cheltenham Spa Town

Gloucestershire
http://www.visitcheltenham.com/

Located on the edge of the Cotswolds region, the Cheltenham Spa Town is one of the busiest and most vibrant destinations in Gloucestershire. It is less than 100 miles east of London. Dotted with regency town house with painted facades, the historic Promenade, the popular Racecourse, and host to a number of Festivals, Cheltenham has become a top tourist attraction in the Cotswolds region.

Cheltenham is named after the River Chelt. It rose into prominence with the discovery of mineral springs in 1716. In 1788, George III came with the royal family to enjoy the hospitality and the spas of the town for five weeks, giving the local spa businesses a huge boost, and making Cheltenham a destination for the aristocrats. So famous are the spas of Cheltenham that not only the city came to be known as Cheltenham Spa Town, even the railway station is named Cheltenham Spa Station. Historic evidence of the popularity of the spas is found in a 1781 Cheltenham Guide that showcased a visit to the town as 'a journey of health and pleasure'.

Another major feature of Cheltenham is horse racing. The Cheltenham Racecourse - http://www.cheltenham.co.uk/ - at Prestbury Park is a major tourist attraction hosting many major races including the Cheltenham Gold Cup, Champion Hurdle, World Hurdle, and the Cotswold Chase. The main racecourse has 2 courses – the Old and the New Course, as well as a cross-country course.

Cheltenham had a booming spa business for half a century – 1790 to 1840. The period saw a sharp rise in the city's fame and fortune, as well as architectural growth. Although much of it has been destroyed to make way for the new, a walk along the historic Montpelier district still has sparks of the old world charm. The Town Hall, located in the Imperial Square, is an early 20th century building that was built in a Victorian style with Corinthian columns.

The Pittville Pump Room – named after Joseph Pitt, the banker who commissioned its construction – is one of the few buildings from Cheltenham's heydays that have remained intact over the passage of time. Built at a cost of £40000 in 1830, the Pump Room is a popular wedding venue today. Interestingly, the spa water is still available as there is an 80 feet deep pump that pumps the water into a fountain in the main hall. Other famous buildings in the area include the Everyman Theatre, the Municipal offices, and the Playhouse Theatre.

The religious revival of the 18th and 19th centuries were reflected through the many churches that were built in the town during this period – the most notable being the Gloucester Cathedral and the St. Mary's Parish Church (listed separately in this section). The steady flow of pilgrims and followers also gave rise to many small businesses and markets in the area making it a popular market town (see Places to Shop section for list of the markets).

Cheltenham has also become a favourite location for films. Other than the Harry Potter movies that were shot in the Gloucester Cathedral, other notable movies shot in the town include The Remains of the Day (1993), The Whistleblower (1993), Pride and Prejudice (1995), and Vanity Fair (2004). Famous citizens of this region include J K Rowling (authoress), W G Grace (cricketer), Gustav Holst (composer), and Anne Robinson (TV hostess).

Cheltenham can be reached through the M5 motorway. The Cheltenham Spa Express is a passenger train connecting the town with London.

Chipping Campden

http://www.chippingcampdenonline.org/

Located off the A44 and A429 motorways, this picturesque town is in the Cotswolds district of Gloucestershire. The name comes from 'chipping, which, in old English, meant market town. The town is regarded 'a gilded masterpiece of limestone and craftsmanship'. It was one of the most important 'wool towns' of the medieval period and saw its wealth grow manifold during the peak of the wool trade in England. The town was established in the 7th century.

Over the centuries, the city has promoted vernacular architecture, as seen through the typical honey coloured limestone buildings along the famous 14th century High Street. In 1970, High Street and many other parts of the town were designated as conservation area protecting the buildings from any major structural changes. Other notable buildings include the 17th century Market Hall, East Banqueting House, St. James's 'Wool' Church, and the early 17th century Alms House.

Chipping Campden was also a centre for the promotion of local (Cotswolds region) handicrafts with the setting up of the Guild of Handicrafts in 1902. The Guild promotes metalworking, furniture making, and wrought ironwork.

The town has a number of gardens, some of which are major tourist attractions – Hidcote Manor, Snowshill Manor, Ernest Wilson Memorial Garden, and the Batdford Arboretum. Tourist attractions also include the Court Barn Museum, Grevel House, and the Campden House & Gateway.

Chipping Campden is chock-a-block with festivals and activities all year round. Popular amongst those are the Music Festival and the Literature Festival featuring artists and participants from even outside England. A popular event in Chipping Campden is the Cotswold Olimpicks dating from 1612, over 280 years before the Olympic Games! It draws athletes and participants from all over England and is a must see if someone is visiting the Cotswolds. The popularity and acceptance of the Olimpicks soared in 1982 after the British Olympic Association recognized it as a part of its pre-history.

Other Tourist attractions in Cotswolds: The British Cotswolds, spread across 6 counties with their numerous medieval towns have several attractions that would take even an avid traveler many weeks to see. Listed below are a few more of the attractions that are highlighted and promoted by Cotswold Tourism.

Nature & Gardens

Batsford Aboretum & Wild Garden

Moreton-in-Marsh
Tel: 01386 701 441
www.batsarb.co.uk

Birdland – Park & Gardens

Rissington Road, Bourton-on-the-Water
Tel: 01451 820 480
www.birdland.co.uk

Clearwell Caves

Near Coleford (1.5 miles south of Coleford town centre)
Tel: 01594 832 535
www.clearwellcaves.com

Cotswold Way National Trail

Fosse Way, Northleach
Between Chipping Campden and Bath
Tel: 01451 862 000
www.nationaltrail.co.uk/cotswold

Westonbirt – The National Arboretum

Forestry Commission
Tetbury
Tel: 01666 880 220
www.forestry.gov.uk/westonbirt

Thermal Bath Spa

Hot Bath Street
Bath
Tel: 0844 888 0844
www.thermaebathspa.com

Stratford Butterfly Farm

Swans Nest Lane
Stratford-upon-Avon
Tel: 01789 299 288
www.butterflyfarm.co.uk

Kenilworth Castle & Elizabethan Garden

Kenilworth (off A46 motorway)
Tel: 01926 852 078
www.english-heritage.org.uk/kenilworth

Historical Cathedrals & Castles

Berkeley Castle

Berkeley (midway between Bristol and Gloucester)
Tel: 01453 810 303
www.berkeley-castle.com

Roman Baths

Abbey Church Yard
Bath
Tel: 01225 477 785
www.romanbaths.co.uk

Snowshill Manor & Garden

Snowshill – near Broadway Village
Tel: 01386 852 410
www.nationaltrust.org.uk/snowshill

Sudeley Castle

Winchcombe – 8 miles northeast of Cheltenham
Tel: 01242 602 308
www.sudeleycastle.co.uk

Tewkesbury Abbey

Church Street
Tewkesbury
Tel: 01684 850 959
www.tewkesburyabbey.org.uk

Museums & Others

Out of the Hat

100 Church Street
Tewkesbury
Tel: 01684 855 040
www.outofthehat.org.uk

Nature in Art

Wallsworth Hall
Twigworth. Gloucester
Tel: 01452 731 422
www.nature-in-art.uk

Keith Harding's World of Mechanical Music

High Street
Northleach
Tel: 01451 860 181
www.mechanicalmusic.co.uk

COTSWOLDS, FOREST OF DEAN & WYE VALLEY TRAVEL GUIDE

Recommendations for the Budget Traveller

Places to Stay

Days Inn Michaelwood

Michaelwood Service Area
M5 J13/14 Dursely
Gloucestershire
http://www.daysinnmichaelwood.co.uk/

Ideal for visitors to the Swindon, Hungerford, and Newbury areas, the 38 guest room Days Inn is ideal for families where children below 12 years stay and eat free.

Berkeley Castle and Cotswold Wildlife Park are nearby attractions. Each en-suite room has free unlimited Wi-Fi, Hypnos beds, and a complimentary hot drinks tray. There is 24hr reception and free parking.

Internet room rates start from £56 for Single and Double rooms. There are dedicated smoking rooms.

The Old Stocks Hotel, Restaurant & Bar

The Square Stow on the Hold
Gloucestershire
Tel: 01451 870 014
http://www.oldstockshotel.co.uk/

This B&B Hotel is housed in a Grade II listed 16th century building made with honey coloured stone, typical of the Cotswolds region. It is located close to Stow-on-the-Wold and Bourton-on-the-Waters. The 18 room hotel also has dog friendly garden facing rooms. There are 2 restaurants with full bars.

Room rates are dependent on the season and events in the neighborhood. Standard rooms start from £36 and Superior rooms from £46.

Byfield House

Bisley Street
Painswick
Tel: 01452 812 607
http://www.byfieldhouse.com/

The Byfield House is the winner of the 2012 Cotswold Tourism Award for Best B&B. It is a Grade II listed 16thcentury building with a historic Tudor Hall, and an 18th century Drawing Room. It gives a feel of the old English charm with its medieval oak door, old rugs, and furniture. It is very close to the St Mary's Church and the Rococo Gardens and 6 miles from the Gloucester Cathedral.

Room rates for the Garden Room and the 2nd floor apartments start from £100 for double occupancy. Please note that there is no facility for credit cards. Rooms have a complimentary selection of food and drinks.

The Battledown

125 Hales Road
Cheltenham
Tel: 01242 233 881
http://www.thebattledown.co.uk/

It is a 5min ride by taxi from the station and close to many of the Cheltenham attractions. The Hotel is housed in a beautiful mid 19th century French Colonial villa. The Hotel has a walled garden and free private car park. All the en-suite rooms are equipped with the basic modern facilities. Room rates start £55 for single occupancy and £60 for double occupancy in a Single Room. Breakfast is included in the room rates.

The Ivy House

2 Victoria Road, Cirencester
Tel: 01285 656 626
http://www.ivyhousecotswolds.com/

The Ivy House is in a late 19th century building that is a 3 minute walk from the Cirencester city centre which has the famous Corinium Museum and the Cirencester Park. It is also close to Stratford-upon-Avon, Cheltenham, and Bath.

The en-suite rooms have all the basic facilities. Room rates start from £50 for single occupancy and £70 for double occupancy.

Places to Eat

Piazza Fontana

30 Castle Street
Cirencester
Tel: 01285 643 133
http://piazzafontana.net/

This eatery, as the name suggests, serves Italian cuisine. It has a cozy warm interior and excellent service. Starters of olives and homemade bread start from £3. Pasta and Risotti are priced between £8 – 10. The non-vegetarian main course starts from £13. There is also a wide collection of Italian wines.

Cutlers Restaurant

Number Four at Stow Hotel
Fosseway
Stow-on-the-Wold
Tel: 01451 830 297
http://www.hotelnumberfour.co.uk/

The Cutlers Restaurant is in the Number Four at Stow Hotel and serves English cuisine. It is located right in the heart of 'captivating Cotswolds'.

The restaurant has a special menu for Sunday Lunch; a 3-course lunch costs £30. There is a wide variety of meat dishes to try from; specially recommended are the lamb dishes. A 2-course lunch cost £15. The restaurant is open from 8:00am – 10:00am for breakfast; 12noon – 2:00 pm for lunch, and 7:00 pm – 9:00 pm for dinner (closed on Sundays)

Lumiere Restaurant

Clarence Parade
Cheltenham
Tel: 01242 222 200
http://www.lumiere.cc/

Winner of Cotswold Life's Restaurant of the Year 2013 Award, the Lumiere serves British food along with seafood and contemporary cuisine. It is located at the city centre and is ideal for a break between shopping. A 3-course lunch menu costs £28, and a 3-course dinner menu costs £49. There is also a wine menu. Lunch is served 12noon – 1:30pm from Wed – Sat, and dinner is served 7:00 pm – 9:00 pm from Tues – Sat. The restaurant is available for private hire on Sun & Mon.

Café Mosaic

The Woolmarket, Cirencester
http://www.cafemosaic.co.uk/

Sandwiches and baguettes have made Café Mosaic a favorite for a quick bite.

A location close to the tourist attractions and a friendly staff contributes to its popularity. The café does not have any franchises in order to keep a control over the quality of food. Soup of the Day costs £4.50. Paella costs £7.95. Wine and desserts are also served. Special menus are served from 12noon for a couple of hours.

Prithvi Restaurant

37 Bath Road
Cheltenham
Tel: 01242 226 229
http://prithvirestaurant.com/

The Indian restaurant has limited seating and it is best to reserve a table. (Note: There is a deposit for seating above 6 people as the biggest table seats up to 8 persons). There is a 5-course set meal costing £35 per person. The 2-course lunch menu costs £12.90. Cuisine is primarily North Indian although there a few dishes from West India. The restaurant has excellent service as it does not book more than one seating per night. There is also a good variety of wine and cocktails.

Places to Shop

Highgrove Gardens

Highgrove Estate, Doughton
Tetbury, Gloucestershire
Tel: 0845 521 4342
http://www.highgrovegardens.com;
http://www.highgroveshop.com/

The Highgrove Gardens are the private gardens of the Prince of Wales and the Duchess of Cornwall. Highgrove employs and engages a team of highly skilled crafts people who make unique products for the home and garden. The Highgrove Gardens have regular tours and it is not possible to visit the shop without having booked a tour of the Gardens. (There are standalone stores in Tetbury, Bath, London, and Windsor) Products, which are also available online, include the Coronation Series of teacups (£55), mugs (£25), and side plates (£39). There are soft toys starting from £12. Most of the products are linked with Royalty or Royal events.

Bath Markets

Somerset

Bath, in the western part of the Cotswolds region has slowly gained prominence as a popular shopping destination.

Major shopping areas include the Artisan Quarter (for independent crafts and curio shops), Southgate (high street brands), Upper Town (jewelry and boutique stores, Western Area (local product and produce market along with the Green Park Station Market), Milsom Quarter (designer stores and high-end shopping centre), and Central Area (variety of stores in the historical part of the town). The Guildhall Market has a wide range of products with some specializing in tea and coffee. There is also a Saturday Farmers Market. Milsom Street won 'Britain's Best Fashion Street 2010' at the Google Street View Awards.

Tewkesbury Markets

Spring Gardens Car Park
Oldbury Road
Gloucestershire

Tewkesbury has a very popular town market with 60 – 80 stalls. Market days are Wednesdays and Saturdays. The three main streets of the town – Church Street, High Street, and Barton Street also have a number of shops selling a variety of products. Popular stores in the town include Dough Boys Bakery, Bikes and Bits, and 1471 Delicatessen. Be there before noon to avoid the rush and to find a good parking spot.

Stroud Markets

Gloucestershire
http://shopinstroud.com/

Home to a number of festivals in the Cotswolds region, Stroud is also a favourite for those who are looking for organic products and local produce from the Cotswolds region – bringing it the nickname The Covent Garden of the Cotswolds. Popular amongst those is the Sunday market held on the first Sunday of every month at the Cornhill market Square and the surrounding streets. The Sunday market has a flea market section and food stalls.

Cheltenham Markets

Gloucestershire

Cheltenham was granted permission by Henry III in 1226 to hold a market every Thursday, a tradition that has been carried on for centuries. One can visit the market on High Street and buy a variety of products, from cabbages to CDs. The Farmer's Market held on the 2nd and last Fridays of each month at the Promenade is a place to buy local produce as well as sample the local delicacies. Antique lovers can try the stores at the famed Cheltenham Racecourse; there is an admission fee of £2. The Sunday Undercover market is held in an underground parking place on Chaman Road; it is open from 8:00 am – 1:00 pm.

Forest of Dean & the Wye Valley

The Forest of Dean in the Wye Valley is an ancient forest which is many hundreds of years old. This was once the hunting grounds of King Henry V (born in nearby Monmouth) and was one of the places where he honed the skills that would allow his army to win the historic battle over the French at Agincourt. This is where William Wordsworth walked and conceived of poetry that has been loved by generations.

The landscape is dotted with small towns that have been around for centuries. Opportunities abound for outdoor enthusiasts, whether on the rivers, walking in the hills or exploring in the forest.

Archaeological digs have provided evidence to show that the region has been inhabited since Mesolithic times. The region marked one of the westernmost reaches of the Roman Empire in Britain, and the forest itself was protected as a hunting ground by the Roman government – a protection it would enjoy through the Tudor period.

In more recent times, the area became known for industry – most notably coal mining, metallurgy and forestry. There are several sites that enjoy international protection for their role at the beginning of the Industrial Revolution. This took its toll on the forest which shrunk in size over the centuries. Today, however, the Forest of Dean and the Wye Valley have been designated as Areas of Outstanding Natural Beauty, which affords them a degree of protection from the threat of redevelopment.

The region straddles the border between England and Wales, and has seen periods of both tension and cooperation between the two countries. Today, visitors will cross between the two countries almost without noticing. You'll enjoy trying to master the pronunciation of the unusual Welsh place names.

Official signs include both the Welsh and English name for a place – and sometimes the two names bear no resemblance to one another.

Location & Orientation

The Wye Valley takes its name from the River Wye that straddles England and Wales. In Wales it crosses the county of Monmouthshire, and in England it extends into Gloucestershire and Herefordshire.

The Forest of Dean is located predominantly in Gloucestershire. It sits on a plateau bordered by the River Wye, the River Severn and the city of Gloucester.

Given the number of small villages and towns, as well as remote locations within the forest, the easiest way to get around is by car. If you will travel by railway to the region, and then hire a car for the duration of your trip, there are major railway stations at Abergavenny, Chepstow, Lydney and Gloucester. Similarly, there are National Express coach stations in Newent, Chepstow, Ross-on-Wye, Monmouth and Gloucester.

For those who'll be entering the UK by plane, the closest airports are Bristol, Cardiff and Birmingham. All three are within a 90-minute driving radius. The London airports and Manchester airport are also viable options despite being further away.

There is a £3.50 parking fee in the Forestry Commission car parks. An annual Forestry Commission Discovery Pass can be purchased for £20 that will allow you to park in Forestry Commission car parks for a year, and it also gives additional perks and discounts on related services.

Please see their website at:
http://www.forestry.gov.uk/pass.

Climate & When to Visit

The region experiences a mild oceanic climate. The hottest months are July and August when temperatures range from 13°C to 23°C (55°F to 75°F). This is also the driest time of year with an average rainfall of around two inches/month. Winter temperatures are typically at their coldest in December and January when they range from 3°C to 8°C (37°F to 46°F). The wettest months are in the spring and fall.

Many of the towns host Christmas markets that attract tourists during the winter.

The stunning natural beauty of the area is present at all times of year, so the best time to visit really depends on when you're free to travel and your personal preferences. You'll find there's much to discover in any season.

Sightseeing Highlights

Forest of Dean

Visitors to the Forest of Dean will enjoy a large array of outdoor activities. Popular hiking trails include the **Wye Valley Walk**, which runs from Chepstow to Plylimon in central Wales and passes through rugged terrain, much of it historically relevant. **Offa's Dyke Path** follows the earthen barrier built by King Offa in the 8th century – which marks, roughly, the border of England and Wales today. The Wysis Way bisects the Forest of Dean, passing through some stunning terrain, and goes through Gloucester into the Cotswolds.

Many will enjoy cycling throughout the region. There are bike trails for all levels, from those suitable for families with children to those for more adventurous mountain bikers. The **Family Cycle trail** follows the former Severn and Wye railway on a ten-mile circle through the forest. Mountain bike enthusiasts will find trails of different grades, and even a set of skills loops to help you develop your abilities and control.

If you aren't traveling with your own bike, you can hire one from Pedalabikeaway Cycle Center (http://www.pedalabikeaway.co.uk/), Dean Forest Cycles (http://www.deanforestcycles.co.uk/) and Forest Bikes (http://www.forestbikes.com/).

If you'd like to explore the Wye Valley from the vantage point of the river that gives the region its name, you'll find any number of canoe and kayak rental shops in the towns that line the Wye's riverbanks. Monmouth Canoe's rates start at £20 for a half-day (http://www.monmouthcanoe.co.uk/river-wye-canoeing/). For £55, Way2Go Adventures in Symond's Wat offers guided half- and full-day trips along the river – and have sea-kayaking tours. http://www.way2goadventures.co.uk/).

There are also places to rock climb, caves to explore with trained spelunkers, a number of zip-line courses to explore the forest canopy and more. Check out the regions website for more details: http://www.visitforestofdean.co.uk/discover/Things%20to%20do/t-1553%7C/

Chepstow (Welsh: Cas-Gwent)

This charming town sits at the lower end of the Wye Valley and serves as an unofficial "entrance" to the region. It's castle was the first built after the Norman Conquest and has watched over the entrance to the Severn River ever since. The town grew up around the castle and has been an important port and market town for almost 1000 years.

Chepstow was once a part of the Wye Tour (at the dawn of the modern age of tourism). Chepstow has long attracted visitors from all parts of Britain in search of romantic landscapes.

The **Chepstow Museum** (Gwy House, Bridge Street, Tel: 01291 625981) recalls the town's history, and the history of the Wye Tour and its influence on the region. It is located very close to the castle.

The **Old Wye Bridge** was built in the early 19th century and is an important landmark today. It is notable for its beautiful cast iron construction – which is difficult to maintain given that it spans the Severn at a point where the river's tide at times rises and falls by 40 feet! The bridge crosses the border between England and Wales. You can stand in the middle of the bridge with one foot in England and the other in Wales.

Caerleon (Welsh: Caerllion)

Not far from Chepstow is the small town of Caerleon. This town is of importance historically as the site of a permanent Roman legionary fortress – one of only three in Britain. Unlike most of the UK's Roman ruins Caerleon's are special due to their size…and because many archaeologists and historians think it may be King Arthur's seat of power. That's right: Caerleon may well be **Camelot**!

Caerleon was known to the Romans in its day as *Isca Augusta*, and it was the westernmost outpost of the Roman Empire in Britannia, a fortress that was inhabited for over 200 years, possibly as late as 380 AD.

Take a look at the remains of the iconic amphitheatre (the most intact in the UK) that once seated 60,000 spectators (almost seven times the number of the current population!). Portions of the fortress wall still survive (despite centuries of locals having taken the stones for their own buildings). The barracks are the best-preserved Roman barracks in Europe.

If you'd like to put the town's ancient sites into some context, visit the **National Roman Legion Museum**. Its permanent exhibition includes many artefacts discovered in the area. It also features rooms reconstructed to look like they would have appeared to the Roman soldiers who inhabited them. There is also a **Roman Baths Museum** where you can see the ruins of the thermal baths where the Roman soldiers would have cleaned up and relaxed after a day of training.

The Arthurian connections trace back to Geoffrey of Monmouth, whose 12th century opus, *The History of the Kings of Britain*, is the first to specify that Caerleon was a place connected to King Arthur. The fact that Geoffrey wrote his book 600 years after the death of Arthur and archaeological evidence doesn't support the theory hasn't stopped subsequent authors from considering Caerleon the site of Camelot. The fact is, there isn't much evidence to disprove the theory either – and it's not hard to imagine the amphitheatre as the famed roundtable. Even if it's not a table exactly, it's still a circular gathering place – perhaps *table* was just a metaphor?

Caerleon hosts an **arts festival** every July. It features tree sculptures from around the world that are displayed all over the town. The festival happens in conjunction with the annual Roman legion battle reenactment that takes place in the amphitheatre.

Tintern (Welsh: Tyndyrn)

William Wordsworth was a notable walker of the Wye Tour. He liked it so much, in fact, that five years later he walked it again with his sister (and best friend), Dorothy. The poems that he wrote during that time period found their way into *Lyrical Ballads*, his collaboration with Samuel Taylor Coleridge. The book marked a dramatic shift in the content and structure of poetry and it ushered in the British Romantic era.

One poem in particular, "Lines written a few miles above Tintern Abbey" – commonly known as **"Tintern Abbey"** – has been taught in schools and universities all over the Anglophone world and is what put the Wye Valley on the map. The ruined abbey exists today in much the same condition as it did when the Wordsworths visited in the late 18th century.

When the Cistercian abbey was built in the 12th century it was the first of its kind in Wales. The abbey saw 400 years of monastic life before Henry VIII dissolved the monasteries and liquidated their assets in the 16th century. The lord of Chepstow sold off lead from the abbey's roof shortly thereafter, putting in motion the centuries of decay that would follow.

Although the abbey is the most famous site in the area, you'll also want to see the **Abbey Mill**. Although it's hard to imagine today in it's bucolic setting, Tintern was once a major industrial area and an important producer of bronzeware. The Abbey Mill is a testament to that era with its ancient water wheel. Today the mill is home to a variety of craft studios and shops where visitors can browse the work of local artists and artisans.

Abergavenny (Welsh: Y Fenni)

Abergavenny is sometimes referred to as "The Gateway to Wales," which is disputable since it doesn't even sit along the border. It is, however, the indisputable gateway to the **Brecon Beacons national park**. The Brecon Beacons mountain range is rocky and stark. The first time you see the mountains, you will begin to feel that the landscape has suddenly become less English and more definitively Welsh – which gives merit to Abergavenny's nickname.

The Brecon Beacons National Park edges up against the Wye Valley and the park has been designated an International Dark-Sky Reserve – which is to say, a place with so little light pollution that you can still experience darkness as our ancestors before the 20th century would have experienced it.

Abergavenny is famous for its **food festival** (http://abergavennyfoodfestival.com/), which The Guardian has deemed as important to the food world as Cannes is to the film world. The festival takes place every September, and if you visit you'll find hundreds of different food stalls, cookery classes, talks, debates, wine tastings, etc. It's held in one of the major market halls in Wales, which is worth a visit at any time of year. Here you'll find an antiques market, a crafts market and a flea market in addition to the daily farmers' market.

Abergavenny has a reputation as a foodie's paradise and you will find plenty of good places to eat no matter what time of year you visit. You can learn about the town's history by visiting its museum, which is set in the ruins of a Norman castle – one of the finest examples of a motte and bailey castle in Britain.

You're also a short drive away from **Blaenavon, a UNESCO World Heritage Site**. Its ironworks had such an impact on metallurgy that similar foundries followed and the Industrial Revolution was begun.

Hereford

Hereford sits along the River Wye on the English-side of the border with Wales. The first thing you'll see towering over the Hereford landscape is its 11th century **Norman Cathedral**. Here you can see the *Mappa Mundi* – a map of the world as it was depicted by a 13th century cartographer. It's the largest complete medieval map and is very important to historians.

You can also visit the cathedral's library. During the medieval period all books were manuscripts (by the Latin definition: *written by hand*). A manuscript as long as the Bible took an incredibly long time to create and was therefore very valuable. In ancient times, books were chained to pedestals to prevent theft as you can see at the library. The cathedral library is one of the largest, best-preserved chained medieval libraries. Here you can see beautiful illuminated manuscripts of the Gospels from the Saxon period.

After spending an afternoon learning about the Middle Ages in the cathedral, you'll be ready for a drink. Hereford is home to the Bulmers Cider company – maker of Bulmers and Strongbow ciders (among others). Hereford is also home to **The Cider Museum** (http://www.cidermuseum.co.uk/ at Pomona Place; Tel: 01432 354207) and **King Offa Distillery** where you can learn all about the history and process of making cider.

Monmouth (Welsh: Trefynwy)

This busy market town sits in the heart of the Wye Valley and lends its name to the surrounding county of Monmouthshire. Although most of the architecture is noticeably Georgian, this was a very important town in medieval times and there are traces of this history still to be found.

Most prominent is the **Monnow Bridge** with its medieval stone gate that is fully intact – the only one of its kind that remains in Great Britain. Its Norman castle, now in ruins, will be of interest to devotees of history and Shakespeare. It was the birthplace of Prince Hal, later King Henry V. The castle also houses a regimental museum.

Also of interest to Shakespeare enthusiasts: the medieval historian Geoffrey of Monmouth is from here. His *History of the Kings of Britain* provided the source material for several of Shakespeare's plays as well as the earliest tales of King Arthur.

Moving ahead in time, **Monmouth's Shire Hall** is an elegant Georgian courthouse and county administrative centre. It's important in modern British history as the site where leaders of the Chartist movement were put on trial in the 1840s. Rulings on this populist movement reverberated through the country and had lasting effects on British democracy.

The **Kymin**, a Georgian banquet hall, sits on the outskirts of town and is the perfect place for you to bring a picnic lunch. Its location atop a wooded hill presents the visitor with incredible views of the surrounding Monmouthshire countryside. Admiral Lord Nelson brought his mistress, Lady Hamilton, here and described it as the most beautiful place he'd ever seen.

Speaking of Nelson, the **Monmouth Museum** has such a large collection of his memorabilia that it is often mistakenly referred to as the **Nelson Museum**. Their collection contains many of his personal letters and his fighting sword.

One of Monmouth's favorite sons of the last 150 years is Charles Rolls. A dashing, aristocratic adventurer, Rolls was an early automobile enthusiast, balloonist and one of Britain's first licensed airplane pilots. He was also, sadly, the first Briton to die in an airplane accident in 1910 at the age of 32. Although his life was cut short, at the time of his death he held the world record for the longest balloon flight and he was the first person to make a non-stop flight across the English Channel. Most importantly, however, is the legacy he left to the automobile world: in 1906 he and his friend Henry Royce founded the Rolls-Royce company.

You can visit Rolls' home, **The Hendre**, which is the best-preserved Victorian manse in Monmouthshire. If you're a golfer, you might want to consider playing at the **Rolls of Monmouth Golf Club** located on the grounds surrounding the house. Visit their website for more information (http://www.therollsgolfclub.co.uk/).

Ross-on-Wye

The picturesque town of Ross-on-Wye sits on the northern edge of the Forest of Dean and is a good place to base yourself to explore the Wye Valley. An easy way to do this is to take a boat cruise. **Wye Valley Cruises** (http://www.wyenot.com/wyecruises01.htm; Symonds Yat Leisure Park, Symonds Yat West; Tel: 07721 895346) launch from the nearby small village of Symonds Yat West and take you on a leisurely excursion down the river. You can also arrange to hire canoes and kayaks from here.

Back in town, take a look at the **market hall**. Built in the 1650s, this red sandstone structure sits in the middle of the town centre and is still the site of a bustling market scene as well as antique stores and artisan boutiques.

St. Mary's Church is built of the same rusty-coloured sandstone as the market hall, and you can see its towering spire from the moment you enter the town. The church is over 700 years old and contains some beautiful medieval sculpted tombs. Outside be sure to take a moment of contemplation before the Plague Cross. Erected in 1637, it stands as a monument to the more than 300 townspeople who died of the plague that year and who were buried hastily – without much ceremony and without coffins – nearby in a plague pit.

Next to the church you'll find the **Prospect**, a lovely garden park that offers some excellent views of the town and environs.

Across the river from Ross you'll find **Wilton Castle**. A popular ruined Norman fortress that is covered in ivy and roses. A walk through its gardens makes for a romantic afternoon spent in a fairy tale setting.

Goodrich Castle, in nearby Goodrich, is of a similar age and in a similar condition as Wilton but is a more imposing structure. Its high walls remind you that castles were built, first and foremost, for defense. This site is maintained by English Heritage and has excellent audio guide to lead you around as you explore.

Usk (Welsh: Brynbuga)

Usk is located on the river of the same name. One of the oldest towns in Wales, this is a quiet town that is known for its horticulturally adept citizens. They've won many awards in the annual **Britain in Bloom competition**, and if you'd like to see why then be sure to visit them in June when the residents open their private gardens to the public. It's a wonderful way to meet some of the locals.

Usk Castle is a ruined Norman fortification, which sits off the beaten path. The entry fee is whatever you care to donate, and their means of counting the number of visitors every day is to have you drop a pebble into a bowl. Once in, you're likely to find yourself as one of very few visitors, so you can enjoy the ruins and the gardens in a quiet ambience.

The **Rural Life Museum** (The Malt Barn, New Market Street, Tel: 01291 673777; http://www.uskmuseum.org/) is a popular attraction. It shows how agriculture changed from the pre-motor times of 1850 to 1950 by displaying hundreds of different tools and machines. Its library is also an impressive collection of books, photographs and records. Before you leave, be sure to get your picture taken with Bessie, a fake-yet-somehow-milkable cow!

Gloucester

Gloucester is a beautiful cathedral and port city located on the Severn. Gloucester straddles two distinct and interesting regions: the Wye Valley and Wales to the west and the ever-charming Cotswolds to the south and east.

Gloucester cathedral dominates the skyline and parts of it have been around since the Saxon era in the 7th century (although most of what you see was built later between the 11th and 15th centuries).

Like most cathedrals and large churches, if you pay attention to the details you'll notice some quirks and eccentricities. Two quirks of note in Gloucester Cathedral are located in its stained glass windows where you can see people playing golf in one of the stained glass windows and a medieval version of football in another. The golf window is particularly puzzling since golf originated in Scotland yet this image is 300 years older.

If you walk around the cloisters and begin to feel like you've entered Hogwarts School of Witchcraft and Wizardry, that's because the cathedral was used extensively in three of the **Harry Potter films**.

After the cathedral, the city is best known for its **Victorian docks**. Although inland, its position on the Severn makes it a perfect river port. A great place to learn about this history is the **Gloucester Waterways Museum**. Once you've learned about the importance of the city as a port during the Victorian era, you can get on the water yourself in one of their many daily canal tours.

Also take a look at **Prinknash Abbey**. Not only do the buildings date from the 11th through the 16th centuries, but there is still an active monastic community living here and following the Rule of St. Benedict – written nearly 1500 years ago. While parts of the monastery are not open to the public, the abbey does welcome visitors to its gardens and it maintains an aviary (with many free-roaming birds) and a deer park.

By comparison with the other towns and villages in the region, Gloucester is quite large and cosmopolitan. It has, therefore, more to offer in terms of nightlife. If you're looking for a fun night on the town you'll find many bars and clubs on Lower Eastgate Street, including Liquid/Diva and The Registry, which are the biggest.

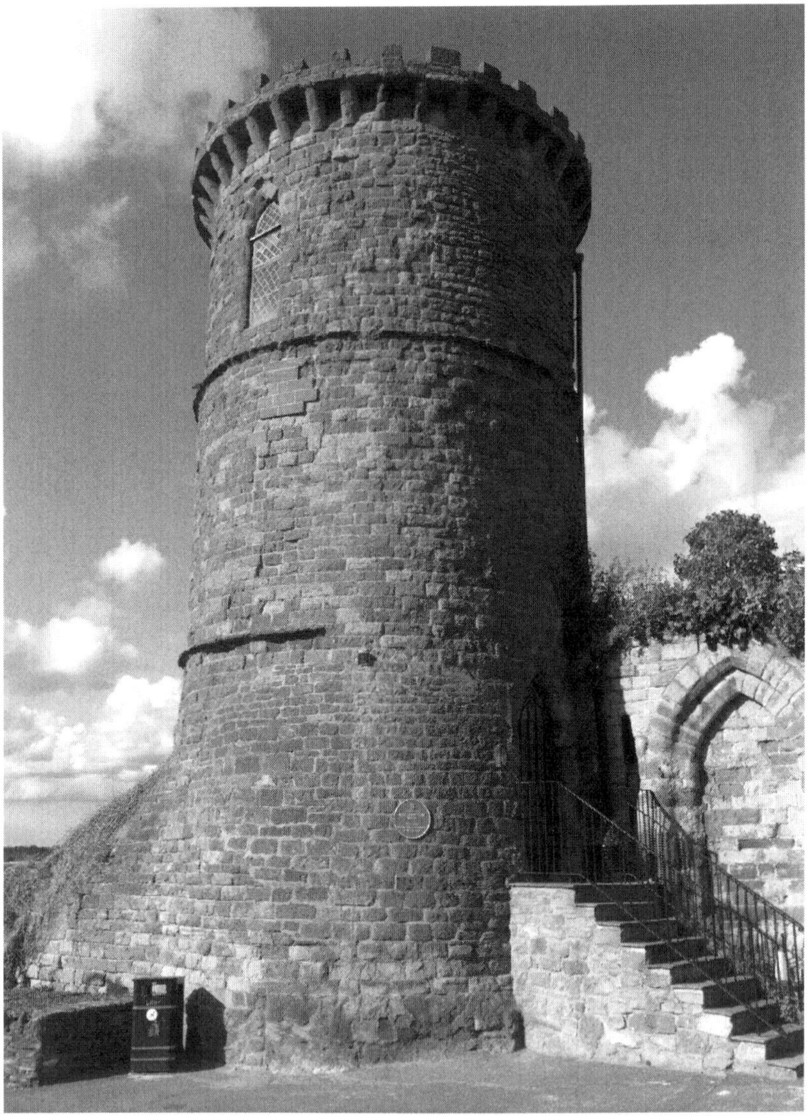

Recommendations for the Budget Traveller

Places to Stay

Hotel Ibis Gloucester

Corinium Ave A417
Gloucester
GL4 3DG
Tel: 01452 623650
http://www.ibis.com/gb/hotel-6900-ibis-gloucester/index.shtml

The Hotel Ibis offers clean, modern rooms at an affordable price (less than £40/night if you book online). If you're driving, you could easily make Gloucester your home base for a few days and travel into the rest of the Wye Valley as a series of day trips. This hotel is located near the city centre, and rooms come equipped with free WiFi, hair dryers and satellite television. There is a restaurant and bar on site.

Castle View Hotel

16 Bridge Street
Chepstow
NP16 5EZ
Tel: 01291 620349
http://www.hotelchepstow.co.uk/

This is a handsome, Tudor house-turned-hotel in Chepstow that enjoys an excellent location directly across from Chepstow Castle. It's a small hotel with only 13 rooms (although the 13th is numbered 14…just to be safe), so be sure to book ahead. If you stay here you'll enjoy seeing the murals and tapestries that have been in the house since the 1600s. It boasts an excellent restaurant and a garden pub. A single room can be booked through their website for £45. Online rates for a double room can be found around £60.

Riverside Hotel

Cinderhill Street
Monmouth
NP25 5EY
Tel: 01600 715577
http://www.riversidehotelmonmouth.co.uk/

This hotel used to be a Victorian coaching inn, but today it's somewhat more elegant and comfortable.

Its 19 rooms vary in size and shape, but all come equipped with Free WiFi access and bathrooms en suite. The hotel restaurant serves both full English and Welsh breakfasts, and visitors can enjoy a quiet evening in the residents bar or a louder, more energetic night watching your favorite team at the hotel's sports bar. Rooms are available for under £60 online, and if you visit the hotel's website you'll find they frequently post special package deals.

Munstone House

Munstone
Hereford
HR1 3AH
Tel: 01432 267122
http://www.munstonehouse.com/index.html

This beautiful country house hotel ought to cost much more than the £50-60 they charge per night (which includes a full English breakfast). Located just outside of central Hereford, this hotel offers the visitor beautiful grounds to walk around with fantastic views of the surrounding countryside. Rooms are spacious and luxurious and come with free WiFi. This is a small hotel with just a few rooms, so book ahead to guarantee your place.

Premier Inn

Ledbury Road
Ross-on-Wye
HR9 7QJ
Tel: 08715 278944
http://www.premierinn.com/en/hotel/ROSTRA/ross-on-wye

This chain offers consistent quality at an affordable price. They offer large, comfortable beds, free WiFi, a television with over 80 channels, bathrooms en suite with hair dryers. This location has a Beefeater restaurant on site. The price for a basic room without breakfast or extra frills is £29, so you really can't beat it. It should be noted, however, that this particular location does not have air conditioner units in the rooms – something to remember if you're traveling in July or August.

Places to Eat

Warwick's Country Pub & Eatery

Llantillio Crossenny, Abergavenny, NP7 8TL
Tel: 01600 780227
http://warwickspub.blogspot.com/

Warwick's Country Pub is a great place to go for both traditional British cuisine and a local pub atmosphere.

Located in Abergavenny, halfway to Monmouth, you might want to make this a stop on your way between these two cities. Owners Sue and Alan will give you a warm welcome and give you tips and ideas about other things to see and do in the immediate area. Check out their blog for events at the pub itself – this place is a very active member of its community. Menu items range from £5-£18.

The Three Salmons

Bridge Street
Usk
NP15 1RY
Tel: 01291 672133
http://www.threesalmons.co.uk/restaurant/

The Three Salmons team cooks with produce grown in the chef's garden behind the building and only uses lamb and beef raised in the area. Traditional Welsh fare using local Welsh ingredients. And you can wash it all down with a pint from their selection of locally brewed ales and ciders. Although steaks can cost over £20, most items on their menu are less than £14, so you're getting great quality at a great price. The restaurant is conveniently located in the center of Usk.

Na Lampang

12 Kingsholm Road
Gloucester
Tel: 01452 382970
http://nalampang.weebly.com/home.html

Na Lampang is a highly regarded Thai restaurant in Gloucester. The cuisine is largely from Northern Thailand, which is known for being less spicy than the south. All dishes are made fresh (with ingredients grown in the restaurant's own garden), and the restaurant has a welcoming atmosphere. Most curries, stir-fries and noodle dishes are under £8; specialties and fish are all under £13. This restaurant has developed a following with a regular clientele – always a good sign.

N68 Bistro

2 Beaufort Arms Court
Monmouth
NP25 3UA
Tel: 01600 772055
https://www.facebook.com/N68Bistro

This bistro offers traditional British cuisine with a flair. Run by a mother and sons trio, their menu changes weekly (and is posted on their Facebook page), but you can always depend on them using the freshest ingredients grown or raised nearby. Everything on the menu is under £10 with the exception of the lamb – good prices for delicious dishes.

Shangri-La

17 Mary Street
Chepstow
Tel: 01291 622959

This restaurant is considered by many to offer the best Chinese food in Chepstow and environs. Its menu includes many familiar dishes, but offers enough deviation from the typical Chinese menu to excite foodies looking to try something new. Due to its popularity, it's likely to be packed when you visit, but the staff is welcoming and will seat you quickly.

Places to Shop

Eastgate Shopping Centre

Eastgate Street
Gloucester
http://intoeastgate.co.uk/home

Eastgate Street is a charming, brick-lane pedestrian thoroughfare that is lined with shops of all sorts. It's shopping centre will meet your needs for clothing, electronics and other goods.

Here you'll find M&S as well as cafes, bakeries and a food court. There is also a large, more traditional indoor market within the shopping centre where you'll find stalls set up by local artisans and foodmongers of various sorts so if the big name stores are not what you're looking for, the market will provide an interesting alternative.

Stella Books

Monmouth Road
Tintern
NP16 6SE
Tel: 01291 689755
http://www.stellabooks.com/

Stella Books is a specialty bookstore dedicated to rare books. Their shelves and storerooms house over 30,000 out-of-print tomes on every subject that range in price from £5 to £25,000. An easy stop to make after your visit to Tintern Abbey – at which point you might be interested in a book on local history. They've got a first edition *A Walk Through Wales in 1797* for £180 or, if that's out of your budget, you could opt for *Gwent Local History* (1982) for £5.

Labels Outlet Shopping

Ross-on-Wye, M50/J4, Herefordshire, HR9 7QQ
Tel: 01989 769000
http://www.labelsoutletshopping.co.uk/

Labels Outlet Shopping draws over a million visitors every year who come for the 200-plus brand names at bargain prices. You'll find all the brands you're familiar with and many smaller labels that you might not have heard of. For this reason, there isn't the kind of cookie-cutter sameness that you might find at other shopping centres. There is an excellent food hall on site – and for any dish you try, you can purchase the ingredients and recipe right there!

Ross Garden Store

Ross-on-Wye, Herefordshire, HR9 7BW
Tel: 01989 568999
http://www.rossgardenstore.com/

Spending all this time in such lush, beautiful outdoor settings is sure to inspire your green thumb. Whether you're a gardening novice or master horticulturist, a stop at the Ross Garden Store is sure to please. It's housed in what used to be a train yard, but today is practically a park of its own. The staff is able to help you locate whichever of the thousands of plants you might be looking for, and what they don't have they'll be happy to order for you. They also sell furniture and statuary to help accent your garden and give it character.

Gloucestershire Arts & Crafts Centre

4 College Street
Gloucester
GL1 2LE
Tel: 01452 307161
http://www.glosartscrafts.co.uk/

The Gloucestershire Arts and Crafts Centre is conveniently located beside the Cathedral. This collective is run by the artists who have made the pieces and products on sale, and you'll have the opportunity to speak with some of the artists themselves. With jewelry, tapestry, wall hangings, and a huge assortment of *objets d'art*, you'll find a wonderful range of unique pieces to peruse.

Printed in Great Britain
by Amazon.co.uk, Ltd.,
Marston Gate.